Blessed to
be a Blessing

Shelley
Thanks so much
for your acts of kindness
Thanks for blessing
my family & I
Much Love
Kim

KIM RIDLEY

Blessed to be a Blessing

IN GOOD TIMES *and* BAD TIMES

Charleston, SC
www.PalmettoPublishing.com

Blessed to be a Blessing

Copyright © 2021 by Kim Ridley

All rights reserved

First Edition

Paperback ISBN: 978-1-63837-703-0
eBook ISBN: 978-1-63837-704-7

CONTENTS

ACKNOWLEDGMENTS

To God who's everything I've ever needed...........He gets all the glory for allowing me to live to tell my story.

To my parents the late Lloyd Ridley Sr. & Frances E. Ridley who are no longer here to witness this monumental time in my life. I'm grateful that you decided to give me life. Even though they're not here I know you'd be pleased. I'm sure they're smiling from heaven and are super proud.

To my praying grandmother who helped raise and covered me in prayer as often as needed. I'm so glad I had a PRAYING GRANDMOTHER who never turned her back on me. I learned how to pray the devil out of my life.

To my children Chadrod R. Brown and Cierra N. Brown I'll never regret having the best of both worlds in the year of 1989 becoming a single mother of a beautiful baby boy March 8th & December 30th.

To my 6 amazing grandchildren Jakai Ashton Brown, Breleigh Dior Brown, Skylar Amia Brown, Riley Shelia Brown Kingston Messiah Brown and Rhyan Ashley Brown. Spending quality time with all of the at the same time makes life grand. I've been able to declare and decree generational curses are destroyed. A legacy of generational blessings will flow to them in Jesus name amen.

To my brother Desmond Lydell Everett. I love you to the moon and beyond. Your love and support for me has been like no other.

To my amazing youngest Uncle Terry Everett who've survived a tragic accident in the year of August 2017. I could be selfish to say "God saved him to be the voice that I've needed during a season of my life. He's been my prophet in trying times. He's here because he still has a God-filled assignment for those who come in contact with him.

To my spiritual mothers Momma Blanche Watson & Momma Rosalee Miller blood couldn't make us closer. Every woman needs a good elder woman who will lead and guide her in all truth. Even when it comes to being chastened. The two of you stepped right in when I needed you the most. I'm forever grateful for your prayers unconditional love, generosity and support.

To Alice Bates you've been the big sister and Angel sent from God above. May God continue to give you the desires of your heart.

To community leaders who've been assigned to the assignment I carry out in the community. It's too many to name. They know who they are..........Together we do it better and win.

I could never express my gratitude to you. We are blessed to be a blessing. Ain't no stopping us now we're on the move. Let's continue to do the work.

CHAPTER ONE

Blessed to be a Blessing!

All of my life I knew there was something inside leading me to help others. Even during the highs and lows of my life, I knew that God has gifted me to be a blessing. I'll use His words throughout my story to make it all make sense. For example, the Bible declares "It is more BLESSED to give than to

RECEIVE." Learning this principle has allowed me to never ever worry about any situation I've had in life.

Most people believe giving is always monetary only. The truth of the matter is, giving comes in many forms. There are gifts and talents that are far greater than money. Again, let me share God's word "Your Gifts will make room for you" (Proverbs 18:16). For the sake of God almighty being who He is and will always be. I'm blessed to be a blessing in so many ways and I've always encouraged myself to be a blessing. Know what you possess within. I've heard many say "I'm trying to find what my purpose is in life. I've discovered spending time alone in the presence of God and putting yourself in His Word helps a great deal.

Listen, as a child growing up as the middle child of 3 girls and one boy, I watched my mother Frances E. Ridley while my father was away serving in the military. She had her hands full with being a good cook, seamstress, stylist etc. She loved to travel and wasn't afraid to make changes of any kind. I watched everything she did and it helped shape me into who I am and I feel like I learned from the BEST.

Why did I just put the word best in all caps. She left a legacy for me to finish what she started.

I'd like to take you through my journey so you can see the price you have to pay to get where God wants to place you in life. Remember I mentioned using the word of God along the way, well, I'm a firm believer "The steps of a good man are ordered by God." (Psalms 37:23). In my case, the steps of a good woman (my mother and I).

My mother was the 3 of 12 children. Born to the late William Cephas Everett and Missouri Everett and she was definitely a blessing to her siblings and those who knew her during her 49 years of life. As a young lady having 2 children of my own, life threw another big challenge at me. My mother was diagnosed with cancer and a mental illness (Schizophrenia) all at the same time. It was most certainly heartbreaking for me because every young woman looks for a mother to rear her in the right direction. (I write this with tears rolling down my face.)

I was definitely blessed to have a mother who, even in her sickness, nurtured the different skills and talents that I have today. She definitely left her mark in her own way...........classy, smart, beautiful, and gifted. I'd never in a million years thought she'd leave this earth at 49 years young. I knew even with all the she went through; I'd be the generational curse destroyer. God would allow generational blessings to be upon me and my children. If I could call heaven, I'd say thanks mom for giving me life and love.

Listen, no matter the challenges you face in your life time, don't back down. Face them and be the conqueror you were called to be.

I remember when I entered high school, my mother urged me to take Home Economics. Especially, since she loved to cook and sew. That's exactly what I did and left high school with some skills that would bless me throughout my whole life. The funny thing that stuck with me is my teacher saying I always did amazing work. This is the classroom I look forward to going every day. When I graduated in May 1988, I received high honors in sewing class. I really desired to go to Fashion Design School in

New York City but I knew my mother didn't have the finances to send me to college.

Graduation happened and not even a year later, I found myself becoming a very young mother of not only 1 child but 2 children in 1989. My son Chadrod Rico Brown born March 8th 1989. Excited for my first child but afraid at the same time to be a young mother. He arrived and all I could do was smile and say look at my MIRACLE and life continued to move on. My son was now 5 weeks, I decided I had to go back to school but this time I would take up cosmetology. I signed up for

Ron Thomas Cosmetology School and life began to feel good again. I had moved with my father and stepmother to be close to school since it was on a bus line.

It was time for me to go back to the doctor for my 6 weeks checkup only to find out I was pregnant again. Now, this was the time I could've almost had a nervous breakdown. I'm like, I just had a baby and the tears start flowing like crazy. Living with my father and having a second child this soon, I knew he wasn't going for this. He was upset I was pregnant so young the first time but he was happy he had his first grandson. Decisions, decisions, decisions...I just had a baby and I can barely take care of myself and him. On one hand, I was happy and thought every mother wants a baby girl. Then on the other, I was thinking, you're going to be talked about even more. My mind was just all over the place. I kept my secret for 3 weeks and things began to get a bit rougher. I had started school at Ron Thomas but knew I couldn't continue. I mentioned my situation to one of the teachers she gave me information on resources single moms with situations like mine. After some research, I found out I qualified by having 2 kids and was able to get assistance from social services.

I moved into a one-bedroom apartment with the help of the Rental Allowance Program right across the street from the school. At that time, I could say I regret keeping my babies but that was not the case. I was a young mother and it was time to sink or swim. There was a time in my life when I was looked down upon for having 2 children at the age of 19 & 20. My son was born on March 8,1989 and my daughter was born on December 30, 1989. My baby girl was definitely a blessing; she arrived on my birthday. Yes, two babies born in the same year. Single mom on social services getting that check and food stamps. Struggling trying to figure out how to make ends meet for my two children and myself at the age of 20 years old. My mother was there for me to rely on her guidance and I was literally having breakdown after breakdown. For months, day and night, I cried out to God asking, "WHY ME?!". One thing I do know, no matter my struggles God never left my side. He is true to His word. (Deuteronomy 31:6)

There was a day I shared my story with a young lady who is struggling with my same story. Listen, I heard her cry like my cry. Now I understand my trials and trauma as a young woman weren't just for me to go through without a plan. We overcome by the word of our TESTIMONY. I know one thing as I continued to minister to this young lady, I made sure she would have a testimony too.

Never judge a book by its cover. You don't know what people are going through.

Single Mother/Married Mother there's greatness in YOU. Don't be distracted, God is able to do exceedingly abundantly above we can ask or think. Remember you are BLESSED to be a blessing.

The early ages of my life had so many lessons. Many will probably regret the choices made they made.

You know as I looked back and reflect on my life, I can truly say "I have no regrets especially being a mother who never gave her blessings away." I truly believe this is the God's way of showing me why I had to go through everything I went through.

Before ending this chapter, I want to leave you with something to think about. My mother was the strongest woman I've ever known. Even in the midst of sickness mentally and physically, she fought like a soldier. I'm reminded about the numerous times she'd go back and forth to the hospital weather it would be for a psychiatric evaluation or a checkup for her breast cancer. All I knew was to pray have faith that God would turn things around for her. If he didn't, he'd grace me to deal with the reality that the Lord God gives and He takes away, but never leave us comfortless. This whole situation caused me to grow up quickly. I don't know how people who still have mothers are not connected to the ones who gave birth to them. Yes, I know everyone have different situations but the Bible tells us to honor thy mother and father that thy days may be long upon the earth. That's some good stuff. The blessing is long life and God's word is true. Someone right now might be saying "You don't know what my mother has done to me. That's why I don't have a relationship." I could go on and on but I'm going to leave this right here. Go mend that which is broken. Forgiveness blesses you. Forgiveness will free you and put you in places you've never dreamed. Forgiveness is really for you.

CHAPTER TWO

Welfare to Gods Fare

Never despise the day of small beginnings. Moving forward with two children, I had to decide where to go from here. Trying to figure out how if I wanted to entertain such toxic relationship with my children's father because I thought I needed his help would be like opening up a can of worms. I passed on that situation because I definitely saw no change in him. One thing I've realized in life, when a person wants to do right and be a part of your life you don't have to force it. Whatever is meant to be, becomes.

Let me take a short detour to give you a snapshot of our relationship. I had to wonder why I would hold on to a relationship that wasn't going anywhere. We both were very young at the time. As people would say babies having babies. Another thing I had to realize is the young man I had babies with was really abusive mentally and physically. We definitely would need counseling. That's one thing he never wanted to do. We were really two people going in the opposite direction.

He was hanging in the streets doing bad things. Every time I'd try to make things work for the sake of having children, it just never did. I wanted my son to have a better example of a good man. I wanted my daughter to be the daddy's girl. Years of coming in and out of their lives was just a NO for me especially, as my son grew older. I didn't want him to see a man abuse his mother and think it was ok to hit women. Another thing I never wanted my daughter to think it would be ok for a man to put his hands on her.

There was a time I had a good neighbor who would look out for my kids and I. She knew when I was going through bad times in my relationship. During one incident a knock on the door literally saved my life. My neighbor had called the police. When they arrived and asked was I ok, my response would be yes, but deep down I was hurting and scared all at the same time to confess the truth of physical abuse.

Listen, listen, listen don't ever try to hold on to anything that's harmful to your mental and physical well-being. I'm reminded of what my neighbor would tell me some days later after we would talk. She'd say baby me tell you something. Love isn't supposed to hurt. "Love is kind/a good feeling of affection"

I'm not telling you what to do, but you must make some healthy decisions for you and your children.

Those decisions became easier as he went back and forth to jail time after time.

Let me just close this subject with some good news. After many years of being a repeat offender back and forth in the jail system, he's now in society and doing well for himself. The relationship with the kids, who are now grown with children of their own, isn't perfect but it's working. We now together have 6 amazing grandkids and share in birthdays and holidays. These are the happy days.

Now back to our original topic…I'm on a leave of absence from school and stuck with a student loan. One, good thing that happened during this time is that other Rental Assistance Program resources became available to me. I met a lot of other single mothers with children who needed help. I could share all the information that was shared with me.

The days of reapplying for social service benefits was absolutely a long day. Sitting in a building your whole day with 2 young babies only to get enough money really for rent, gas & electric and maybe a telephone bill. I wanted to scream especially because the social service building waiting space felt so claustrophobic. The workers took all day getting paperwork done. I would cry out to God to please give me a break!!! I know I was definitely the cause of my situation but help me make the best of what I've caused in my life at present. Ok, not only did He do it. Like they say "HE DID THAT"

I've always kept my appearance up and before leaving the building I had so many compliments about my hair. Now after 3 ladies asked me where did you get your hair done? My response was "Me, I did it." Next question would be where do you do hair? I responded, "My house." One young lady "Can I get your phone number?" I was very hesitant because you know we were always taught everybody couldn't come in our house.

At any rate, that was the BINGO for my next source of income. I hadn't even finished school yet. That was something else to think about. I didn't want to get in trouble operating without my cosmetology license. Watching my mother at a young age and the natural ability (the gift) for doing hair began to pay off. Even though I wasn't making a lot of money. I was making enough to make end meet and take care of my children.

God will give you increase at the appointed time. My family and friends knew I'd started doing hair at home and my clientele started to grow by word of mouth. I began to meet some real good people.

Another door opened for me by way of the Baltimore Postal Service, where my father was a supervisor.

One good thing about the job, I was able to make enough money to have proof of income to move to a 2-bedroom apartment. "THANK YOU JESUS" I'm back to making life changes for the better and feeling blessed. My whole dream was to finish what I started. You might ask "What was that?" Being the stylist that I know should be.

I continued to do hair while working at the post office and met a lady there who became a client. I called her church lady every time I talked to her. She invited me to come visit her church and one day I decided to go. I mentioned to her not having a car to get there and I wasn't catching no bus with my two small kids. She did offer to give us a ride and bring us home. That particular Sunday was youth Sunday. Well, you want to know how being in the right place at the right time BLESSED me. My babies even enjoyed the service especially the choir singing and shouting. Now listen, I was reared by my praying grandmother when my mom became ill. My grandmother stepped up and helped my mother with us.

The church thing wasn't new to me I just had to find my way back especially since I was raising my kids alone. God always made ways when there seemed to be no way.

There are times when you have to step up to the plate and make things happen. Leaving stress behind and pushing forward making things happen. I used the system when I needed to but the bottom line is, I came right back and poured right back into the system when I got on track. It's been a good feeling to know the once was and the now. Praises be unto to God who gave me the victory.

CHAPTER THREE

Sharing a small space

I f walls could talk..........These are some of the things my walls would say. I'm not going to tell it all but I'm definitely going to tell on it. Forgetting those things which are behind me I press.

Now knowing and beginning to trust in the Lord and leaning not to my own understanding, life becomes a bit clearer and easier to handle. Putting God first has changed me and my way of thinking. I ran into a young lady who was struggling with just one child after moving to the same apartment complex. I couldn't just watch her struggle like I did. Being kind-hearted, I allowed her to move in with me and my kids in this 2-bedroom apartment. What was I thinking?! I was thinking with my heart and definitely not my head. We were packed in that place like sardines.

Things had really begun to frustrate me because I needed more space. I thought about how I could get myself out of what I had gotten myself into for the sake of trying to be a blessing to someone. I started finding things to do so I'd only really be home to eat and go to bed. That's definitely not how you want to live in the space you call home.

I was praying daily for directions. I've always had a prayer life and relationships with God so know His voice. That's how I've been able to maneuver my way through life. The small space made me believe that I'd really appreciate the new space that was up ahead. Counting my blessings after I'd blessed someone else.

CHAPTER FOUR

Purpose, Power, Praise

(Know Who You Are)

Listen, listen, listen know that everyone has a divine purpose. Many know what their purpose is and while others are still seeking to it. Well in this chapter I'm sharing with you the different ways I had to get to know myself. There are times I tried to search within to realize what purpose I have on this earth. I had two babies in one year, had to leave cosmetology school, involved in abusive & toxic relationships, my mother died at a young age, moving year after year (7 times) as a young woman. This can't be life for me. The truth of the matter is God does all things well and much of my pain produced my purpose. God took me through all of that so in all these areas I could be a blessing to someone along my life journey. As they say you can't have a testimony without a test.

Life can make you or break you. I remember falling on hard times once again. I met another guy just as nice as he could be and had a lot to offer but in a very wrong way. He had a job but was also a drug dealer. I believed as long as he kept that part of the outside business away from my kids and I, things would be good. We started dating and he did so many nice things for my kids and me and brought a lot of nice things for me. It was time for me to move once again considering the Rental Allowance Program grant was about to expire. I needed to upgrade my living arrangements.

The kids were getting older. Having a boy and a girl sharing the same room with me because I allowed someone else who was in dire need to stay with us. Things needed to shift in my life.

One day I mentioned to him I needed to find another place to live. He told me "If you find a place, I'll co-sign for you." My jaw literally dropped. Again, I told you he was definitely a nice guy. I immediately started to look for a new place for my kids and I to start the new season of our life. Not long after I found a better area to live in with more space. A nice 2-bedroom, where the kids and I could have our own room. I was blessed by a client who was getting rid of bunk beds during the time I was moving. March 1, 1991 would be my move in date and was just in time for me to give my son a party for his 3rd birthday.

This man was good to me and I had no reason to believe I was being manipulated into having my house be used as his stash house. Of course, if he asked me, that would have been heck to the NO!! I discovered the set up by accident.

I could've kicked myself in the butt for not realizing this man had brought trouble to my door. I say this because there was a day, I came home from working at the salon and my 3-year-old mentioned my boyfriend cooking something in the kitchen. Mind you, he never cooks at all. The inspector gadget in me went looking for details of what was cooking. After looking in the refrigerator and there was no meal prepared, I thought to myself, do I question him or not? After a few days of letting things go. The question comes up, "What did you cook the other day?" His whole facial expression changed. To make a long story short, he was cooking CRACK COCAINE in the house when I was gone. Jesus help me!! Well let me tell you when you are designed for purpose, God will always give you a way of escape. It was a Sunday morning and my client that I spoke about earlier called me and asked me was I coming to church. I definitely needed something to clear my mind. I hesitated but got the kids and I dressed to go to church. Low and behold the message was just me "YOU HAVE TO KNOW WHEN TO LEAVE THE PARTY..........THERE'S PURPOSE in your life".

Listen, listen, listen! When there's PURPOSE & DESTINY on your life, no devil in hell can hinder the plan of God. Thanks be to God I had a praying grandmother and knew enough to call on the name of Jesus in times of trouble.

I wanted to hurry and tell this man he had to take his drugs and leave, but in reality, the place wasn't just mine because he had co-signed for the apartment, so technically it was his place too.

Where would my kids and I go? Even while enduring the consequences of bad decisions in life, the power of God will give me a way of escape. It's a good thing when you're able to come out of something that could've very well destroyed that which God has set up for your life.

Then there's this scripture that tell us "No weapon formed against you shall prosper. (Isiah 54:17) Everything in life set before you, good or bad, you have a choice. Knowing how to pray and commune with God helped me escape from what I got myself into. My prayers were soon answered when my boyfriend was incarcerated for drug distribution and I was able to be free from that world that I never wanted to be involved in anyway. I was able to raise my kids without being in fear. Now let me close this part on a high note.

After serving 5 years in prison. He's now still that same good guy with his own contractual home improvement business. (Romans 2:11) God has no respecter of persons. We are good friends to this day.

Blessed to be a blessing to those in our community.

I'm praising God because I'm not finished with my assignment yet. I'm becoming what God has created me before the foundation of the world. Let me quickly put a praise on who I'm stepping up to be. See the Bible assures me in Jeremiah 29:11, For I know the plans I have for you.

From the outside looking in, you would think that everything I was going through was meant to set me back, but they have really been a SET UP for my life's journey. You have to know everything God has spoken over your life shall come to pass. Please get this in your mind, there's greatness in you. Even if nobody tells you, believe it with everything in your heart.

CHAPTER FIVE

Gods Gifts & Amazing Grace

The number 5 is considered to be God's goodness and grace of God. The grace, love, and mercy of God never runs out for any of us. I'm reminded that every decision made in life was my choice. Whether, I communicated with God or not, His amazing grace found me.

Owning a hair salon really allowed me to share the many gifts God placed upon my life. After, moving yet again because I needed another place and more space for the kids who were getting older and growing and needed their own personal space. I was also trying to get my whole life together by continuing to go to church. I wanted to be an example of how God could change your mess into a message. My clientele consisted of women young, middle aged and older, and I knew my life experiences could be a blessing to them all.

I could teach young girls between the ages of 5-18 many things I learned as a young girl growing up. Life teaches us so many things through our good and bad decisions. The good thing is when we become older, we can help the younger make wiser decisions leading and guiding them because we've been through it. This way of thinking led me to establish the Miracles-N-More Christian Charm Academy. The academy taught classes on etiquette, health, hygiene, social graces, public speaking, community services as well as some fun stuff modeling. We would meet for 10 months, every Saturday and have fashion shows, prayer breakfast, and practices for what would lead the young ladies to a grand MiraclesN-More Charm School Cotillion Ball. That magical day would have me in a world wind to make sure everything would go well. My Royal Rubies ages 5-8 would be all dressed up in red gowns, my Pink Ice ages 9-13 would be in pink gowns and the Dazzling Diamonds ages 14-18 women be the oldest group dressed in white gowns.

The night would include family friends and local Business owners who would donate throughout the charm school year. We had presentations from Barbara Robinson of the house of delegates.

Dinner, dancing, photos, and award presentations throughout the entire amazing night. Our young ladies who would leave due to aging out would receive a scholarship in memory of my mother the late Frances E. Ridley. I remember even when I hosted the Miracles-N-More Christian Charm Academy This was a mentoring program for young ladies ages 5-18.

The first year of the academy, I actually raised the funds myself for every young girl who participated. We had 55 young ladies signed up. Without grants people donated money, food, and whatever, was needed to make this God inspired program a success.

One spectacular moment for me as well as for the students, we were able to perform in a historic moment during the Martin Luther King Jr. parade hosted by Baltimore City. Our Dazzling Diamonds, Precious Pink Ice & Royal Rubies gave a phenomenal performance from the step squad within the program led by Raven Montgomery.

God graced me to give back too many young ladies who needed me on so many levels. Graduates would come back to help mentor the next generation of girls coming through the academy. Some would even come back to let me know how what they learned in the academy helps them to this day which blesses me beyond measure. If you know there's a gift in you to make someone happy or make a difference, do it. The world needs more of that. I'm happy when I see others happy.

I did not do this all alone. There have been some phenomenal women in my community who would volunteer time to help rear the young ladies. I was about to name names but there are too many to name and I don't want to leave anyone out. They all know who they are and the purpose by way of being connected to the call. Operating in many gifts led to success stories for these ladies in more ways than one.

CHAPTER SIX

The Return
Finish What you started

I needed a change and this change wouldn't happen in Baltimore, Maryland. Some people fear change, but believe it or not, change is good. Life has so much to offer out there, but people get stuck in their familiar ways. Sometimes, it's God's desire to change your story.

In 2012, I met a sister that I never knew I had. Before my father passed away, he came to my house to tell me about her and asked would I want to meet her. I told him sure. She came in from Atlanta and I introduced her to my children and grandchildren over dinner. My father was hesitant in wanting to introduce her because he thought I may not accept her as my sister. I've learned that you can't reject people based on face value because you may be missing on a setup from God.

She told us how she found me and made the connection to our father. I tell you the power of the social media platform, Facebook is an all-time best people locator. As time went on, we began to build on our relationship. I invited her back for Thanksgiving and this time she would stay here at my house instead of the hotel. We talked about me being a stylist and how I could bring my skills to the ATL. Well, she had couple of connections and said I could come to Atlanta and meet the right people and start a new journey in the cosmetology field. I took two trips to Atlanta and the second trip was the BINGO for me.

I met a guy who was the head hair stylist for Tyler Perry stage plays. You talking about super excited. We talked and he told me to get back here as soon as I can. He was telling me he took a look at my work on my Facebook page and how my skills would work for the big city and screen. You know all I could think about is leaving everything I knew in Baltimore behind and getting my big break.

They call Atlanta "Black Hollywood." It definitely sounded a bit exciting to me. I was so excited for the opportunity but had lots of anxiety about telling my children and my clientele, whom I had been servicing for 15 plus years, I was leaving.

My children were grown by this time, so when I told them about the move my son Chadrod said, "Ma
I'm not going. I'm not leaving my son". As a mother I was blessed to know how he felt about leaving. Especially, since his father walked out of his life many times. He actually went out found an apartment on his own. The big blessing for him because I was leaving everything except my clothes. He was able to have his apartment furnished from the house.

My daughter Cierra was like Breleigh and I are coming with you. To start fresh with my daughter and granddaughter was exciting. Getting packed and ready for change. The journey was set to begin and I had to leave the distractions behind and move forward.

Before I left I promised my clients was that I would come back once a month for 3 days to service them.

Talk about a traveling stylist. I'm reminded of the long bus rides and the flights from Baltimore to Atlanta. Jesus take the wheel that definitely took a toll on this body of mine.

I am so glad that I kept the promise to my clients in Maryland, especially since the things didn't happen like I planned. Working with the stylist I mentioned earlier was not what I expected. It seemed like he was working against me more than with me. I couldn't believe I had uprooted my life for nothing. I thought back to the last Sunday before leaving Baltimore. I remember going visit the church where my granddaughter Skylar was christened Faith Christian Fellowship World Outreach of Owings Mills, Maryland. The word was so rich and the choir was certainly amazing. I went to shake the hands of the Pastor and First Lady and told them how I enjoyed the service from start to finish. If I was staying in Maryland, I would've made this my church home. The pastor responded with "Well if it doesn't work out you can always come back and do just that." I was so adamant about not coming back home to Maryland but only to visit I didn't pay take his words seriously.

As I reflect on every moment moving and returning. Life sometimes takes us back full circle. There was a mission and ministry in coming back. Besides, when things didn't go as planned, I'm glad the door to come back to was opened. Moving forward on the next phase of my life mission

CHAPTER SEVEN

Together we do it better and win

I n seasons of my life God sent "DESTINY HELPERS".
He prepares visionaries and sends those whom will to
help carry out the vision. I'm reminded that to everything
there is a season.
Ecclesiastes 3

1 For everything there is a season, and a time
for every a purpose under heaven:

2 a time to be born, and a time to die; a time
to plant, and a time to pluck up that which is
planted;

3 a time to kill, and a time to heal; a time to break
down, and a time to build up;

4 a time to weep, and a time to laugh; a time to
mourn, and a time to dance;

5 a time to cast away stones, and a time to gather
stones together; a time to embrace, and a time
to refrain from embracing;

6 a time to seek, and a time to lose; a time to
keep, and a time to cast away; 7 a time to rend,
and a time to sew; a time to keep silence, and

a time to speak; 8 a time to love, and a time to
hate; a time for war, and a time for peace.

The return to Baltimore was strategically planned and
purposed by God. When there is an assignment upon
your life you must recognize it and go with God.

There were many things placed in my hands for an outreach assignment before I left Maryland. There were
many people attached to the assignment. After reconnect-
ing and reconstruction, I had to reach out past supporters
and putting programs back together so I could come back
to finish what I started.

You can never run away from what God has ordained.
Calling all of my clients to let the know I was coming
back home was a blessing and a miracle all at the same
time. Especially, when I would receive back 75 percent
of my clientele to start. Having a place to walk right into
styling without a problem.

You see this is why it's so important to have a good
character and integrity. There was no struggle to walk
back into Hair Town to get my salon chair back.

As the days and weeks progressed, I started thinking of
ways to get back to helping those in my community.
Miracle-N-More had developed many ways to give back.
More than just a salon it became ministry through everyone who decided they wanted to be a part of something
good.

Miracle-N-More was a way to start giving back in more ways than one. It blessed those in our community who are homeless, sick and shut in, kids going back to school and even those who are out of a job. It was nothing for me to ask and receive donations from clients, family, friends and local businesses. That's when I created the motto "Together we do it better and win" I am my sisters' keeper.........Say it with a bag" was birthed out of my desire to help those in the community. We will talk more about that in the chapter 9. The start of the handbag movement continues to this day. Never despise the day of small beginnings. I say this because, one day I was asked to share what I do for those on an interview on WJZ Channel 13. Never one for the camera but I knew this would open up the door for more people to be blessed and more people to donate. After the interview would come another BINGO. The phone rang off the hook and the donations would flow and flood even greater. It would be so much of everything coming in that I had to create what was called a Miracle Closet for all of the donations for the homeless and less fortunate.

Let me share some good news with you. Since the beginning of 2016, we've collected and given out over 3000 handbags filled with toiletries in the city of Baltimore, Maryland. Even to partner with My Sisters Place Women's Shelter.

One day I was preparing to do a mission prayer breakfast for My Sisters Place. My oldest granddaughter Breleigh Dior Brown wanted to get involved and do a dance presentation for the ladies that particular day. We had a glorious time serving 80 homeless women with food, clothing and handbags filled with toiletries. To God be all the glory. Later that day riding home my grand-daughter said to me "Me-Me how come the kids didn't get anything" There was a big sigh and I didn't have an answer at the moment but came up with a solution for the problem.

We decided she would do an "I am my little sisters' keeper". That was an interview waiting with her name on it. The fact that kids watching can also be a bless-ing and learn to be good to others. Ain't no stopping us now............we're on the move and this this movement means everything to me. We take pride in our commu-nity making sure we treat people like we would treat ourselves.

You know God has said in His word the assignment to serve is so great. (Matthew 20:28) just as the son of man did not come to be served but to serve and to give His life as ransom for many. You have to really have a servant's heart for any kind of ministry. The good thing about returning and picking up where I left off, the assignment became easier. God realigned people and things and being obedient to do the work became easy. Let's Go Destiny Helpers.

CHAPTER EIGHT

Destiny Helpers

Every Assignment ordained by God will have a purpose. People will be purpose driven to help carry out the vision. Though the vision may tarry (we sometimes have to wait with patience) it will come to pass.

Considering the number eight means new beginnings, everything I'd do would never start with less than eight people in my circle of any assignment.

I know and have known for many years the gifts and call on my life. Never desired the big platforms but to just work when and where ever God would call me to. I never remember reading about Jesus having a platform anywhere He traveled. He had 12 disciples who He knew that would preach and bless others without a hidden agenda. The fact of the matter is, I know that I could never carry the vision alone.

Jesus Calls Twelve Apostles to Preach and Bless Others
Matthew 10:1-5

> 1 And when he had called unto him his twelve disciples, he gave them power against unclean

spirits, to cast them out, and to heal all manner of sickness and all manner of disease.

2 Now the names of the twelve apostles are these; The first, Simon, who is called Peter, and Andrew his brother; James the son of Zebedee, and John his brother;

3 Philip, and Bartholomew; Thomas, and Matthew the publican; James the son of Alphæus, and Lebbæus, whose surname was Thaddæus;

4 Simon the Canaanite, and Judas Iscariot, who also betrayed him.

Jesus knew who would finish with Him and He Jesus also knew who would betray him.

Everything I put my hands to do, God would send the "Destiny Helpers" to me. These are the many community assignments held together with the "Destiny Helpers"

Miracles-More Hair Salon Inc. Miracles-N-More Women's Ministry, Miracles-N-More Christian Charm Academy, Miracles-N-More Community Outreach. You see there are many things that God will assign to you. I could never take credit alone for everything that has been done, I needed DESTINY HELPERS. The joy of putting smiles on faces of those in need makes me happy.

It makes me glad to know that God is also proud. The word tells us in John 14:12, "Verily, verily I say unto you, He that believeth on me, the works I do he do also; and greater works than these shall he do; because I go unto my father."

The word gives us instructions to follow so where He leads me, I shall follow. Those who follow the lead will definitely be blessed also. I'm a firm believer that everything attached to me wins because I've attached myself to God's purpose. By the way, if you're reading this book consider yourself a Destiny Helper. I'm sowing seed for every copy sold. As a community outreach leader, I've always been in it to win it. The assignment is bigger than me. It's always been for God's glory but it works for my good and the good of those around me.

I'm so grateful for every day. Having God in every aspect in my life to be able to give back without struggling or much thought. Many know my story and have stay connected to the vision. Not me but the purpose. Where there's unity there is strength.

CHAPTER NINE

I am My Sisters Keeper

One day going into my closets I developed a since of saying to myself. This doesn't make any sense. Handbags, handbags and more handbags. To collect as many as I had over the years and only having 5, I actually carry cause me to shake my head as I looked at all the purses that would fall out of my middle spare bedroom closet was like be a hoarder. Every woman has something that they collect that's more than enough than they need. For me it was a season to declutter. I thought to myself there's something I could do other than taking them to goodwill.

BINGO, here is another way to pay it forward to women in need.

I'd fill the handbags and give them out to women I'd see in the street with nowhere to go.

After, talking about it in the salon my clients would say "Are you still collecting handbags for women?" My response would be "Yes I am." It was on and poppin after that.

As women, we know the importance of feeling "BEAUTIFUL" ready to meet the world. Giving these women filled handbags helped to give them that sense of beauty and hope.

As fast as I was receiving, was as fast as we'd find women in need. One good thing about having an outreach ministry, when people who know you and know how effective you are in the community, they will have no problem with giving. I could be in a supermarket and be spotted by someone and hear them yelling "Ms. Kim, I saw you on the news it's a good thing you're doing. How can I donate to the cause?

Sometimes, I'd get in the car with tears of joy. The urgency to make things happen for those in need would be so heavy. I'd be making calls in the middle of the night. Making sure the next drop offs would be bigger and better for those in need.

One of the best days was when we turned giving up a notch. The Miracle Closest was full to overflowing with clothing, coats, shoes, blankets and the filled handbags. I partnered with different organizations around the city to give back in a huge way.

I remember meeting a guy named Nathaniel Fields while making a drop off to My Sisters Place shelter in downtown Baltimore. I just had a quick conversation which led to learning about the nonprofit organization he was a part of Downtown Partnership. Learning and knowing the resources they had to offer could continue to keep me afloat and helping as many people as possible.

I had tv interview along with other prominent community leaders that lead to me volunteering to support the organization "JOY (JUST OUR YOUTH)

BALTIMORE". The director Lonnie Walker hosted a big Thanksgiving dinner for the homeless and less fortunate in our community. Doing that interview together allowed us to raise money, receive gift cards, handbags, toiletries, coats, shoes, blankets to give away during the Thanksgiving dinner. We would sacrifice having dinner with our families to be a blessing to others. The day came to give back. The smiles came and expressions of gratitude came from those we were able to bless. After feeding the people, my outreach volunteers set up a FREE pop-up shop for all genders. This was such an amazing event and I, along with everyone involved, felt privileged to be a part of something that brought so much joy to so many people.

The holidays always seem to bring out the best in people. Wouldn't it be something if we could have that same mindset all year long?

God will line you up to bless you to bless somebody else. Your meal barrel will never be empty. He knows the heart and every intention of man. The giving movement have continued in more ways than one. Take a look at what takes place in the next chapter.

CHAPTER TEN

Evolve or Perish in the midst of a Pandemic

As the year 2019 closed, and we entered 2020 with the world was counting down with great expectation.

Three months into the year, March 23, 2020 to be exact, the US basically shut down due to the COVID-19 pandemic. Major companies' shutdown offices and folks were losing their jobs. Schools, salons, bars, visits to nursing homes, no concerts, and even church doors would have to be closed. I'm saying really, The Church?! That's when having a relationship with God had to kick in. Your faith had to become greater or fail.

At this point pretty much everything except essential hospitals, convenient stores, grocery stores, gas stations would be the only thing that would be open. There would only be minimal of people that could go into these places as instructed by the Governor and or the mayor.

I'm asking myself what now, after many rewarding years of being in the cosmetology field as a salon owner/ stylist. What would be a major crisis could have really had me depressed and at risk of losing everything, BUT GOD.

As days go on, I was thinking maybe this is time off I've needed but I still have bills to pay. I had packed up salon equipment and other items to do hair at home. As I'd been watching and staying caught up on the news of this deadly virus. Fear started to set because by now staying away from people other than the people who you lived with would be strictly ordered. It was mandatory the start of everyone would have to wear a mask everywhere when leaving our homes.

Listen, real life was becoming a live movie. Watching the news was constantly to keep up with this COVID-19 crisis was unbearable. I decided to turn my attention to lay and pray.

One day I received a phone call from very good friend of mine. She said Kim "What are you doing?" I said I'm just laying here. My friend said, "I was just thinking, don't you sew." My reply "Yes". Funny thing is I was wondering how did she know this. She would say why don't you make mask. You could sell them.

I'm thinking to myself, "Yeah, I could but I haven't sewn in many years. Besides, I don't even own a sowing machine." She would go on talking and in the back of my mind was strategizing. After, hanging up I realized I had some Baltimore Ravens material from actual hand sewing some Baltimore Ravens bow ties for my RaveNEttes Women Fan Group. I went in the closet and saw that I still had couple of yards of material I hadn't used.

I figured making masks couldn't be that hard especially when I was the bomb at sewing back in high school.

Wow, thank God for the gift and paying attention in Clothing/Home Economic class. After more than 25 years, the skills I obtained would be a blessing to the world, as well as another source income for me.

After googling how to make mask, I would need a sewing machine, more material, pins etc. I called everyone I thought would have a sewing machine and out of the 12 people I called, Ms. Wendy Prioleau was the life saver. Cutting out the pattern and remembering the measurements would be the easy part. No time to waste, it was time to get to work. After the initial first small batch, I had issues with the sewing machine Panic mode set in, because first this was not my machine and second, where was I going to get another sewing machine to finish making masks. I was talking to my friend and she asked how everything going. I let her know that I was having problems with the machine and she told me that she had to go out in in a little bit and she had something that would help me out. She came with a donation to move forward in what God had started. There was enough money for a new machine and more materials that I needed to finish what would be a huge assignment for the world in crises.

Getting myself together heading out to purchase a brand-new sewing machine. Omg, I'd never in a million years thought a sewing machine would be like finding a needle in a haystack. Going to every Joann Fabric Store and Walmart in my area, Lord help me. After 3 Joann stores and 4 Walmart stores, I found the one and only Singer sewing machine. Only a God could do something like that for me. He's just good like that............Amen Somebody!!!!!

My family and the world had need of my gift. Let these hands become a blessing to those who are in need. I never knew I'd be a blessing to over two thousand faces for protection from a virus that would cause so many to die.

One of my biggest concerns were the children. One day I'd seen a mother with a mask on but not the child. How alarming that was to me? Continuing to get my thoughts together on what and how I could help those children in the world let alone the community. I started off with kid friendly patterns. Knowing that the theme FROZEN was popular. Spider-Man for boys would be a hit. Paw-Patrol for the little boys between the ages of 3-6 would definitely pique the interest of the kids.

By now I was definitely on to something. Just trying to figure out a way to distribute the FREE, yes, I said "FREE," kid friendly mask. I contacted with the local news stations to get the word out to parents who needed masks for children. The plan was to contact Principals at the surrounding schools in the community because breakfast and lunches were still being served.

We were able to give away over 2,000 masks for the kids in the community. We would give out bags filled with a mask, juices, fruit snacks and chips. Making stops throughout the city delivering the "We care.......We can" kid friendly bags made me smile every time and it took my mind off not being in the salon.

The testimonies from people all across the world receiving the mask were phenomenal and brought tears to my eyes. You can visit my Facebook page (Kim Ridley) and you'll see the testimonies the many faces

I've covered in the midst of the pandemic.

CHAPTER ELEVEN

Mask Mania

Your gifts will make room for you
(Proverbs 18-16)

The power of social media still amazes me. Some use this platform for many reasons and during this COVID-19 crisis it has most certainly worked in my favor. The all day and late night sewing in my dining room would become a supply and demand that the world needed.

One thing I knew I had to tackle first was to sew a seed and bless those who were in dire need. The front-line essential employees I knew. I couldn't imagine enduring the long hours in a hospital and working in the stores that over time would become mandatory. I was also able to give masks to the front-line postal employees. Mask Mania for me was in full effect. Cutting countless mask from adults to children size mask; solid patterns floral prints, camouflaged and even character patterns for children. All of this production was happening in my dining room. After posting my work on social media, the orders would begin to pour in like nothing I would ever imagine. God yet again opened up another door for me to be a blessing and definitely to be blessed.

After, what would be a time to sew my seed of free. The sales to those who purchased the masks was through the roof.

Ok, as orders came rushing in, everything I needed, God made happen. Trying to sew and get to the post office weekly had become crazy. Well wouldn't you know, God sent someone to offer to go to the post office for me. All I had to do was give the day and time. They even paid for the postage. Together we do it better and win. Adjusting to what would be our new normal, it's football season and of course every football fan wanted the Baltimore Raven mask. The fabric store couldn't keep them in stock. Then comes breast cancer awareness month which has special meaning to me. I wanted to do something for breast cancer survivors. Getting together a local Breast Cancer Walk in memory of my mother. I'd make over 50 head-wraps and mask sets. We'd raise the money for local women who needed help to survive breast cancer. Blessed to be a blessing in more ways than one. I'm going to be honest to say only a God can use you like He uses me to do the ministry when you take time to hear His voice.

Some days I look back with tears of joy wondering how I've made it this far. Then I realize "being confident knowing He that has begun a "GOOD WORK" in you/ me will carry it on until the day of Christ. We just must be willing to do it work.

CHAPTER TWELVE

Legacy Leaver

I'm reminded that every time I look into the eyes of my 6 beautiful intelligent grandchildren. The generational curses of lack, betrayal, sickness, defeat, destruction, hate, malice, envy, jealousy have been destroyed. It's time to build legacy. Everything, I've done and will do will continue even after I'm gone. I'm a legacy leaver, not only for my children and grandchildren but to the community where I live. They in turn, will carry out the work that's been started. I decree an declare generational blessings over their lives. God made me a promise as He did Abraham. "When Abraham was ninety-nine years old, the Lord appeared to Abraham and said to him "I am Almighty God walk before me and be blameless.

You see, God's word still remains the same and true. We are blessed people because God never changed His word concerning us. We are the seed of Abraham. Many may not know because they lack or don't know God's word. Now in reading some of my life story about blessing and being blessed, I pray you get some of these principles so you too can bless somebody else. Remember it's not only monetary. A smile on your face walking into the dark building where somebody is depressed is a blessing. A loaf of bread for some who has no food to eat is a blessing. Teaching the young morals and respect is a blessing. Leave something valuable to somebody so they can realize it's definitely more blessed to give than receive.

I'll also leave this nugget with you. There will come a time when the seeds you have sown will cause bountiful harvest. Sometimes in ways you weren't expecting. I'm not done yet. I'm just getting started.

Leading the way for the generations to come. There's an open invitation for you to come join me. Let's write the vision and make it plain, though.

ALL ABOUT THE AUTHOR

Kim Cassandra Ridley, was born December 30, 1969, to France is Elaine Everett and Lloyd Ridley Sr. in Harford County Md. She attended Harford County Public high schools (Magnolia Elementary/Yorkwood Elementary Magnolia Middle and later graduated from Joppatown High school)

As a child she was raised by her mother with the help of her praying grandmother while her father traveled in the military. As a young girl she had many talents. She was always a go-getter. Wanting to pursue a career in FASHION DESIGN. Then exiting high school in 1998. She'd later become pregnant having 2 children in the year after graduating. There was a change of plans with many talents and gifts. She went to Ron Thomas Cosmetology School. After getting pregnant with her second child. She couldn't finish school but later finished and received her cosmetology license through apprenticeship at CHIC BUTT UNIQUE HAIR SALON 3844 Crestlyn Rd. in Baltimore off of the Almenda.

Then on to the next salon Act One Hair and Nail Salon. Where she would finish her apprenticeship. Not even a year later. Kim would move on to owing and operating her salon called Miracles-N-More Hair & Nail Salon 3844 Crestlyn Rd. in Baltimore Md. In 1998 the journey would begin.

Now she is the director of the Miracles-N-More Outreach Ministry. Which provides resources for the homeless and less fortunate families in the community in which she lives. Kim was presented with a citation by Delegate Barber Robinson. Also in 2017 Kim received the Mayor's Business Recognition Award hosted by the Greater Baltimore Committee.

She's had many interviews with the local news station Channel 2 & Channel 13 with the movement of the "I am my sisters keeper.........Say it with a bag. She given away over 3000 handbags filled with toiletries, clothing and shoes to less fortunate and homeless women in the community.

She's a living example of an over comer. Overcoming all the odds that were against me as a single mother, welfare recipient, abused physically and mentally by men who I thought loved me. Trying to figure out the right way to go in all of life decision making.